LEFTY

The Story of Left-Handedness

By Marguerite Rush Lerner, M. D.
Illustrated by Rov André

MEDICAL BOOKS FOR CHILDREN

LERNER PUBLICATIONS COMPANY
MINNEAPOLIS, MINNESOTA

International Standard Book Number: 0-8225-0005-1
Library of Congress Catalog Card Number: 60-14007

Third Printing 1963
Fourth Printing 1965
Fifth Printing 1967
Sixth Printing 1967
Seventh Printing 1969
Eighth Printing 1971
Ninth Printing 1975

FOREWORD

This book has been designed to answer a question: what is left-handedness? It meets a specific need of certain children within a group. When a child feels different, he begins to ask why. At the age when left-handedness becomes noticeable, it becomes a matter of comment for other children. When a child can be made to feel that his difference is not an individual one but a general one, and that this difference is interesting, he likes being different. This book is not only reassuring to the left-handed child but also interesting to the right-handed whose curiosity has been aroused.

MYRA E. FOSTER
Assistant Professor in Education
Southern Connecticut State College
First grade teacher
Roger Sherman School, New Haven

C O N T E N T S

WHAT IS LEFT-HANDEDNESS ?

Some people are right-handed. Some people are left-handed. If you write and draw, eat with a fork or spoon, sew, or throw a ball with your left hand, then you are left-handed. If you do all these things with your right hand, then you are right-handed. Some people can use both hands equally well. They are ambi-dextrous.

Are you left-handed? Do you know somebody who is left-handed?

Lefty was a boy whose real name was Seth, but everybody called him Lefty because he was left-handed.

When Lefty was a baby only 6 months old, he reached for toys with either hand. Sometimes he stretched out his right hand to grab a rattle. Sometimes he stretched out his left. When he was 1 year old, every time he wanted a cooky he held up his left hand and said, "Cooky."

When he was 1½ years old, if his mother put a spoon in his right hand, Lefty switched the spoon over to his left hand. And that was the way he ate.

When Lefty was 2 years old, his father brought him a music box from Switzerland. On the right side of the box was a handle. Lefty had to turn the box around and upside down in order to wind the handle to make the music play.

Once when Lefty was 5 years old, he held out his left hand to be polite when his mother introduced him to a new baby sitter. The back of Lefty's left hand got all mixed up with the palm of the baby sitter's right hand. After that, Lefty held out his right hand while saying, "How do you do."

When Lefty went to school he learned to write with his left hand. He could write just as clearly and just as quickly as the right-handed children in his room at school. Lefty's teacher, Mrs. Conn, was right-handed. She held her paper on the desk parallel to her right arm so that the left side of the paper was down and the right side was up. She *pulled* her pencil away from her body as she wrote from left to right.

Lefty held his paper parallel to his left arm so that the right side of the paper was down and the left side was up. He *pushed* his pencil toward his body as he wrote from left to right.

Like many left-handers, Lefty found it easy to write backwards, from right to left. Once he tried to play a trick on his teacher. He wrote backwards, and Mrs. Conn had to hold the writing up

to a mirror to make the letters look like forward writing.

"Lefty," Mrs. Conn said, "did you know that our alphabet, the ABC's, began thousands of years ago with people who wrote from right to left? Today, however, we write English from left to right."

Lefty asked, "Is anybody in the school left-handed besides me?"

Mrs. Conn said, "Of course. About 5 pupils in each classroom are left-handed. Some teachers say that more children going to school now are left-handed than there were 30 years ago. Perhaps this is because many parents and teachers today believe in letting each child use the hand that seems best for him."

When Lefty was 9 years old, he liked baseball, cowboys, soldiers and Indians.

Lefty could pitch a baseball so well with his left hand that the batters were afraid when he stepped up to the pitcher's mound. When Lefty tried to pitch with his right hand, the ball didn't go where he wanted it to. Lefty laughed, "This isn't my right hand. It's my wrong hand!" And he went ahead and pitched a fast curve with his "southpaw."

Lefty liked to watch baseball games and cowboy programs on television. He found out that many good baseball players were left-handed. Some batters were switch hitters and could hit a ball with either the right hand or the left.

On the cowboy shows, Lefty saw some cowboys draw their guns with the right hand, others with the left. There were even cowboys who could make a fast draw with both hands from right and left-sided holsters at the same time.

Lefty didn't mind being left-handed. But he wanted to know *why* he was left-handed. His mother and father were right-handed. THEIR mothers and fathers (Lefty's grandmothers and grandfathers) were right-handed. But his Uncle David was left-handed. Maybe that had something to do with it.

WHAT LEFTY LEARNED AT THE MUSEUM

Lefty's Uncle David told him that although most people are right-handed, 10 to 20 people out of every 100 are left-handed.

Lefty and Uncle David went to the museum to see what they could find out about left-handed people and left-handed tools.

They saw pictures of soldiers holding guns in the right hand. Lefty asked the museum director, Mr. Hall, "Are there any left-handed soldiers?"

Mr. Hall laughed. "Yes. I am left-handed, and I used to be a soldier. A left-handed person can shoot a gun with his left hand just as well as a right-handed person can shoot with his right hand. But during the American Revolution, when soldiers shot with a flintlock, it was safer to shoot right-handed.

"First the flintlock was loaded with gun powder. Then a wad of paper and a round, lead ball were rammed down the barrel. The flash-pan on the right side of the gun was primed with powder. When the trigger was pulled, a piece of flint held in the hammer scraped against steel, making sparks that dropped into the flash-pan. The flames from the burning powder shot through a hole from the flash-pan into the barrel of the gun, firing the powder in the barrel so that the bullet was pushed out. Not all of the flames shot into the gun. If the flintlock were held against the soldier's right shoulder, some of the flames from the flash-pan burst into the air away from his face. If the gun were held in the left hand against the left shoulder, a soldier might get his nose burned."

Lefty asked, "Do you have any pictures of left-handed soldiers?"

"No," answered Mr. Hall. "But we have copies of pictures

that were painted by a left-handed man who was one of the greatest artists and scientists that ever lived. His name was Leonardo da Vinci."

Lefty saw a copy of a picture that Leonardo da Vinci had painted and of an airplane that he had designed 400 years before the Wright brothers built the first airplane in 1903.

Leonardo da Vinci was a mirror writer. He often wrote backwards just the way Lefty wrote when he tried to trick his teacher.

After Lefty looked at a sample of Leonardo da Vinci's writing, he saw an exhibit of people who lived 100,000 years ago.

Mr. Hall told him, "That time of history was called the Stone Age because the tools used for hunting and fishing were made of stone or flint. The stone tools were shaped by chipping. They could be used with either the right or left hand. It is possible that during the Stone Age just as many people used the left hand as the right.

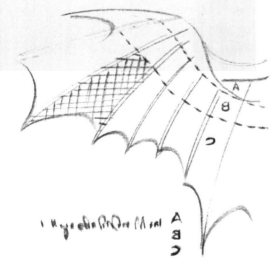

"One thousand years after the Stone Age, man developed the metal, bronze, by fusing copper and tin together. The tools that have been found from this period of history, known as the Bronze Age, were designed more for use by the right hand than the left. It seems that beginning with the Bronze Age there were more right-handed people than left-handed."

When Lefty turned a corner, he saw a suit of shining metal armor—the kind worn by knights 500 years ago.

Mr. Hall explained, "Two thousand years before the knight lived who wore this heavy plate, soldiers fought with swords and bows and arrows and protected themselves with shields. Some people say that the soldiers of ancient times, like Alexander the Great, carried their shields on

the left side of the body to cover up the heart. The left hand held the shield, and the right hand was free to throw a spear or swing a sword. Warriors may have taught their children, down through the ages, to use the right hand to fight with so that the left hand could carry the shield to protect the heart. Alexander the Great himself was left-handed."

On the way home from the museum, Uncle David said, "To-morrow I will take you to the university to meet my friend, Dr. Foster. Dr. Foster is a geneticist. He studies the way certain traits or characteristics are inherited or passed on in a family. If a mother or father has red hair, the genet-icist can figure out how many of their children will have red hair instead of black or blond or brown. Perhaps he can tell us why people are left-handed."

WHAT LEFTY LEARNED
AT THE LABORATORY

Dr. Foster was working in his laboratory at the medical school. He was glad to talk to Lefty. He explained that left-handedness is more common in some families than in others.

"Left-handed mothers and fathers may have more left-handed children than right-handed mothers and fathers. But this isn't always so. Many left-handed parents have right-handed children, and many right-handed parents have left-handed children. Children who inherit a tendency to left-handedness may become left-handed, especially if their mothers or fathers do not try to change them.

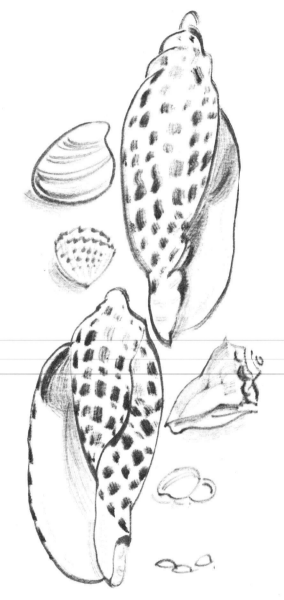

"Also, if a mother is left-handed, the child may copy her. But left-handedness isn't simply a matter of doing what your mother —or father or uncle—does because some children keep on being left-handed even when their parents try very hard to make them use the right hand. Twins, who seem alike in almost every other way, may not favor the same hand. It seems that left-handedness comes from two things—what you have inherited and what you have learned."

Dr. Foster suggested, "Let's talk to Dr. Montagna. He is a biologist. He knows a lot about plant and animal life. Maybe he can tell us whether any animals are left-handed."

Dr. Montagna knew a lot about animals and also about flowers and fish. He showed Lefty two climbing plants which grew in different directions.

"Here is a honeysuckle. See how it twists the way the hands of a clock turn. This is almost rare in plants.

"Here is a morning glory. It twists in an opposite direction or counterclockwise. This plan of winding is the most common in plants.

"There are right and left-handed lobsters and right and left-sided flounders. Most snail families are right-handed. Some are only left-handed. Rhesus monkeys and chimpanzees use either paw for a simple task such as reaching for food. When they are given harder jobs to do, when they have to learn to find their food in a certain place, the monkeys and chimpanzees use one paw more than the other. But just as many monkeys use the left paw as the right."

Dr. Montagna looked at Lefty. "In the plant and animal kingdoms there is right and left-sidedness just as in people."

A NEW GAME

On the way home from the medical school, Lefty said, "Uncle David, will you play a game with me?"

"What kind of game?"

"Let's try to find out the names of all the left-handed people who did something great."

"That's a good idea," said Uncle David. "How should we begin?"

"I want to start with baseball," said Lefty, "because that's what I know something about. Ted Williams and Stan Musial are left-handed hitters. Warren Spahn is a left-handed pitcher. Were there always good left-handed ball players?"

"Yes," answered Uncle David. "There are even men called Lefty, like Lefty Gomez and Lefty Grove. Carl Hubbell, a champion pitcher, was a southpaw. Ty Cobb, a great player, batted left-handed. As a matter of fact, the left-handers really have the edge in baseball."

"What do you mean?" asked Lefty.

"A left-handed batter is closer to first base than a right-handed hitter is. As he bats from left to right, the force of his swing helps send him on his way. Lefty, when you are pitching, do you have any trouble keeping your eye on a runner at first base?"

"No. I can watch a man on first a lot easier than the right-handed pitchers can. Do you know why a left-handed pitcher is called a southpaw?"

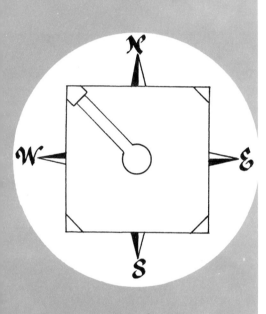

"Baseball historians say that the word southpaw comes from the pitcher's position in the field. Most major league ball parks were laid out so that the sun did not shine in the batter's eyes. The batter faced east or northeast. The sun, which was in the west in the late afternoon, usually shone in the eyes of the rightfielder or leftfielder. In the early days most batters were right-handed and the rightfielder had the least chances in the field. Parks were built so that ordinarily the rightfielder would be the only player to face the sun. The pitcher in such parks had his left hand to the south. When a left-handed pitcher threw the ball, he was using his southpaw."

"That's interesting," said Lefty. "Are there any left-handed people in other sports?"

Uncle David laughed. "Any? Why, there are many. In tennis the Davis Cup was named for Dwight Davis, a left-handed player. Many good tennis players today are left-handed. In fencing some of the best fencers in the world are left-handed."

Lefty asked, "Were any artists left-handed besides Leonardo da Vinci?"

Uncle David thought for a minute. "There were the famous Renaissance painters — Raphael, Hans Holbein, Michelangelo, a sculptor as well as a painter — and the modern artist, Picasso."

"What about writers?" Lefty asked.

"Did you ever hear of *Alice's Adventures in Wonderland* and *Through the Looking Glass?*"

"Yes," answered Lefty, "but I don't know who wrote those stories."

"Lewis Carroll did. He was an author and a mathematician who was left-handed and very interested in mirror images."

Lefty asked, "Do you know if there were any famous left-handed soldiers besides Alexander the Great?"

"Many left-handed fighters were mentioned in the Bible. Charlemagne was left-handed. So was Marshal Foch, the French commander in World War I."

"What about left-handed kings or presidents?" asked Lefty.

"King George VI of England was left-handed. One of the best known southpaws was the 33rd President of the United States — Harry S. Truman."

Lefty said, 'I bet there are a lot of famous left-handers that we don't even know about."

Uncle David said, "Lefty, we almost forgot a left-hander who was one of the greatest baseball players that ever lived—a champion hitter and pitcher."

"I know," shouted Lefty. "Babe Ruth!"

"Yes," Uncle David smiled. "So you see, being left-handed puts you in good company."

"That's great," said Lefty. "I didn't think much about it before, but I'm kind of glad I'm a southpaw."

ABOUT THE AUTHOR

Marguerite Rush Lerner, M.D., was graduated from the University of Minnesota, where she earned a B.A. degree in English literature. She attended Barnard College, studied medicine at Johns Hopkins and Case-Western Reserve universities, and completed her clinical training at the University of Michigan and University of Oregon hospitals. Dr. Lerner is a professor of clinical dermatology at Yale University School of Medicine. She is also a prolific writer of children's books, with some 15 titles to her credit.

We specialize in publishing quality books for young people. For a complete list please write

LERNER PUBLICATIONS COMPANY

241 First Avenue North, Minneapolis, Minnesota 55401

152.3 Lerner, Marguerite
LER   Rush

        Lefty

DATE			
1B			